Don't Scratch, Max!

Written by Judy Nayer ■ Illustrated by Kersti O'Leary

MODERN CURRICULUM PRESS

PROJECT DIRECTOR: Susan Cornell Poskanzer   PRODUCT MANAGERS: Christine A. McArtor
    Leslie A. Baranowski   Denise Smith
EXECUTIVE EDITOR: Wendy Whitnah
ART DIRECTOR: Lisa Olsson
DESIGNER: creatives nyc, Inc.

Published by Modern Curriculum Press

MODERN CURRICULUM PRESS
13900 Prospect Road, Cleveland, Ohio 44136

A Paramount Communications Company

This edition is published simultaneously in Canada by
Globe/Modern Curriculum Press, Toronto.

ISBN 0-8136-1352-3 (STY PK)   ISBN 0-8136-1353-1 (BB)   ISBN 0-8136-1354-X (SB)

2 3 4 5 6 7 8 9 10 97 96 95 94

Max had the chickenpox.
He had spots on his chin
and spots on his nose.

He had spots on his fingers and spots on his toes.

His chin itched. His nose itched.
His fingers itched. His toes itched.

The next day, Max still
had the chickenpox.

He had spots on his arms
and spots on his face.

He had spots on his legs
and spots every place.

His arms itched. His face itched.
His legs itched. Every place itched!

The next day, Max still
had the chickenpox.

He had spots on his elbow
and spots on his knee.

Yikes! Max had spots everywhere he could see!

His elbow itched. His knee itched. Yes, everywhere he felt itched!

The next day, Max still had the chickenpox.

But he felt much better.
Then Max found a brand-new spot.

Now his sister itches a lot!